T0194024

A HAUNTING BIRTHDAY PARTY

WRITTEN BY TINA NYKULAK RUIZ
ILLUSTRATED BY ISHIKA SHARMA

AuthorHouse™
1663 Liberty Drive
Bloomington, IN 47403
www.authorhouse.com
Phone: 833-262-8899

Because of the dynamic nature of the Internet, any web addresses or links contained in
this book may have changed since publication and may no longer be valid. The views
expressed in this work are solely those of the author and do not necessarily reflect the views
of the publisher, and the publisher hereby disclaims any responsibility for them.

Any people depicted in stock imagery provided by Getty Images are models,
and such images are being used for illustrative purposes only.
Certain stock imagery © Getty Images.

This book is printed on acid-free paper.

ISBN: 978-1-7283-6617-3 (sc)
ISBN: 978-1-7283-6618-0 (e)

Print information available on the last page.

Published by AuthorHouse 08/28/2024

authorHOUSE

A Haunting Birthday Party

by Tina Nykulak Ruiz

Hi everybody! My name is Harry Pitts, and I would like to tell you about a fabulous birthday party that I went to, with my best friends, Drew A. Blank and Artie Fischel.

It was the week before Halloween, and a bunch of kids from school were asked to meet at the Ray Zen Restaurant. They were going there to celebrate the 9th birthday for Reece A. Roni and his twin sister, Peppa Roni, and everyone was asked to wear a costume.

Peppa Roni made sure to invite her friends - Annie Howe, Callie Flower, Ella Mentry, Rhoda Booke, and her sister, Rita Booke. Her brother had also invited his friends - Alex Blaine Later, Brighton Early, Dan Druff, Howie Doohan, and Stan Still.

And because they all knew each other, they were having a howling good time together.

At a small table off to the side, Judge Mental and his wife, Judy, were celebrating their 50th wedding anniversary. The handsome couple were being pleasantly entertained by all that was happening in the restaurant, and they couldn't help but giggle at how bewitching the children looked in their Halloween costumes.

Kitti Letter was the waitress for that side of the room, and as soon as she saw how many people were sitting in her section, she let out a devilish squeal. "I'm going to make sure that everyone has a spook-tacular evening," she stated happily.

Because the birthday party was for children 12 and under, Kitti made sure to hand out the correct menu. "You each get to pick two items from the first section and one desert," she said kindly. Then she listened as they oohed and awed at everything they were reading.

HALLOWEEN MENU

RAY ZEN RESTAURANT

TOXIC MAC N CHEESE	$3.50
WITCH'S HAIR WITH LICE AND LARVA	$3.50
GOBLIN GARLIC BREAD	$2.00
GRAVEYARD BURGER	$3.90
STAKE AND FRIES	$4.95
MOLD AND MILDEW QUICHE	$3.00
SCREAM OF TOMATOE SOUP	$2.50

DESERTS ARE FREE

RICE CREEPIES

MICE PUDDING

BOO-BERRY PIE

ZOMBIE DROOL

BAKED SPIDER LEGS AND ICE SCREAM

After the waitress took their orders and walked away, Mrs. Mecca Roni stood in the center of the room and began to read a story.

"Two children accidentally stumbled upon an old witch in a dark forest," the mom said in a scary voice. "She lived alone in a gingerbread house covered with chocolates and colorful candies, and she invited them to eat as much as they wanted. But moments later, she grabbed them with her bony fingers and dragged them inside."

Everyone had been wide-eyed with worry during the story, and Mr. I. Ball was more than grateful when it finally ended.

The manager of the restaurant thanked Mrs. Roni for the gruesome tale of Hansel and Gretel, and then it was his turn to speak. "Welcome to the bone-chilling party for Peppa Roni and Reece A. Roni. As a surprise, we have asked our friend, Walter Melon, to perform some magic tricks for you."

Everyone cheered with delight.

Fifteen minutes later, Miss Turi, the head chef at the Ray Zen Restaurant, announced that the frightful food was ready to be served.

The manager thanked the magician, and then asked the children to wait patiently for their Halloween meals to arrive.

The children were fascinated by all that was put on the table, and after they had wolfed down their oddly-named menu items, the manger's girlfriend, Pam Pyer, came out with a beautiful cheesecake. "I want to thank all you ghouls and goblins for making this event so fang-tastic!" she announced proudly. "Now, let's sing the Happy Birthday Song."

When every last crumb of the delightful desert had disappeared, colorful ribbons were torn off and the presents were ripped open. The gifts were playfully inspected, the monster-themed birthday cards were read out loud, and a heartfelt thanks was given to everyone for their kindness.

By 8pm, the kids were tired, so they all made their way to the large double doors at the front of the restaurant. Mr. Roni gave the cashier his money, and after Eve Ning thanked him, she turned to the children. "Cats say meow, ghosts say boo, and I say Happy Halloween to all of you."

Everyone giggled, and seconds later, the large group disappeared into the eerie blanket of night.

The twins had so much fun being with their friends, that it was hard to get them tucked into bed. But after they had settled down and fallen asleep, Peppa Roni and her brother, Reece A. Roni, dreamed about going trick or treating together next week.

As the moon cast a gentle light on their young faces, the children agreed that the magic of Halloween wasn't just in the costumes or the candy, but in the joy of sharing spooky adventures with friends and family. And with their hearts full of laughter and plastic containers full of treats, they whispered goodnight to the stars and closed their eyes.

"Sleep tight, everyone, and remember, there's magic in all of us."

I'm Harry Pitts. Thank you for reading The Haunting Birthday Party. See you next time!

Did you get the double meaning of everyone's name? For those of you who didn't, here's the cheat sheet so you can impress your friends when it's their turn to read this book.

Hairy Pitts	hairy (arm) pits
Drew A. Blank	drew a blank
Artie Fischel	artificial
Ray Zen	raisin
Peppa Roni	pepperoni
Reece A. Roni	Rice a Roni
Annie Howe	anyhow
Callie Flower	cauliflower
Ella Mentry	elementary
Rhoda Booke	wrote a book
Rita Booke	read a book
Alex Blaine Later	I'll explain later

Brighton Early	bright and early
Dan Druff	dandruff
Howie Doohan	how are we doing?
Stan Still	stand still
Judge Mental	judgemental
Kitti Letter	kitty litter
Mecca Roni	macaroni
Mr. I. Ball	eyeball
Walter Melon	watermelon
Miss Turi	mystery
Pam Pire	vampire
Eve Ning	Evening

Printed in the United States
by Baker & Taylor Publisher Services